# Firefighters

Written by Robyn Opie
Photographed by Russell Millard

# Contents

- **Community Helpers** 3
- **Recruits** 4
- **Training** 6
- **Clothing** 8
- **Fire Trucks** 9
- **Equipment** 10
- **First Aid** 12
- **Testing Equipment** 14
- **Rescue** 16
- **Fire Investigation** 18
- **Other Jobs** 20
- **Education** 22
- **Index/Glossary** 24

# Community Helpers

Firefighters are important workers in the community. They help people every day in many ways.

# Recruits

Firefighters have a lot to learn before they go to a real fire.

One of the things they learn is what it is like to be in a burning building.

They also need to be fit and healthy.

# Training

It takes a lot of training to be a firefighter. They learn how to use and take care of their equipment.

Firefighters must get to a fire fast to save people, animals, and things. So they practice using their equipment and getting ready quickly.

Firefighters are trained in first aid, so they can help people who are hurt.

7

# Clothing

Firefighters wear special clothing made from a material that does not burn easily. This special clothing protects them from heat and flames. Around fire and smoke, they use air tanks and masks to help them breathe.

# Fire Trucks

When firefighters respond to a fire or other emergency, they travel in a fire truck or in an ambulance. Flashing lights and sirens help them move quickly along busy streets. Other traffic must move out of their way.

# Equipment

Fire trucks have many places for storing equipment. Firefighters need fire hoses, ladders, and tools such as an ax and a hydrant wrench. The ax helps them enter a burning building when it is locked. It is also used to cut open a roof to let out smoke. Firefighters use the hydrant wrench to turn on the water at a fire hydrant. The water then fills the fire truck.

Sometimes they use special machines that find gas leaks. Too much gas can make a person ill or cause a big explosion.

11

# First Aid

Fire trucks carry a first-aid kit with medical supplies such as bandages and oxygen. They also carry other medical aids such as blankets and splints. Blankets provide warmth to people. Splints protect broken bones by keeping limbs straight and still.

13

# Testing Equipment

Firefighters spend a lot of time testing their equipment. Their equipment must work when they need it at a fire. They test all of the fire hoses and ladders. They refill fire extinguishers and air tanks.

15

# Rescue

Firefighters save people who are trapped in fires. They save homes, buildings, and forests by putting out fires. They help find people who are lost. They also rescue pets and other animals.

New firefighters use dummies to practice their rescuing skills.

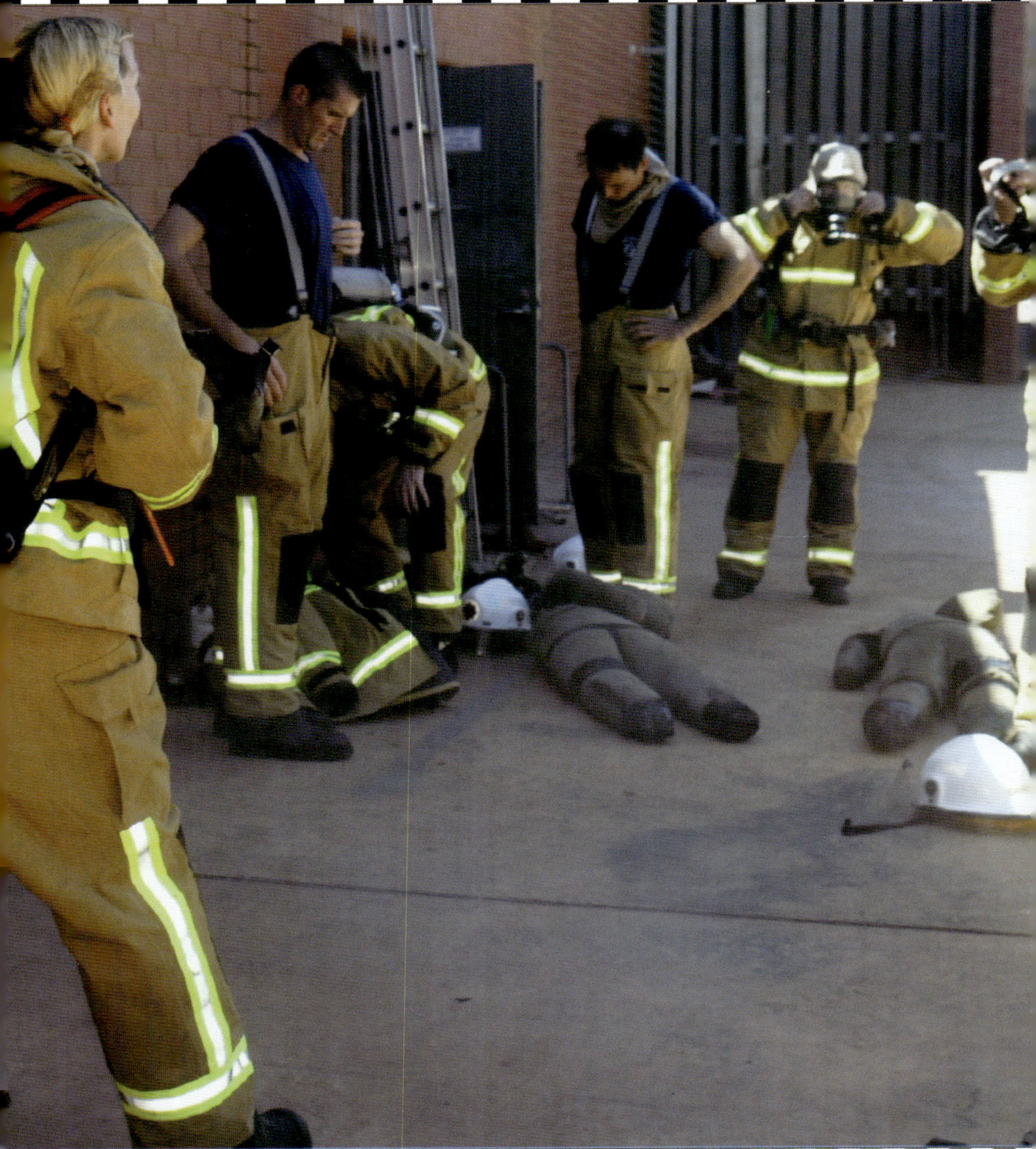

# Fire Investigation

After a fire, firefighters with special training search the building. They can tell how a fire started by studying the burned remains. They can tell if the fire was an accident or not. Some chemicals, like gasoline, burn very easily and are sometimes used to start fires.

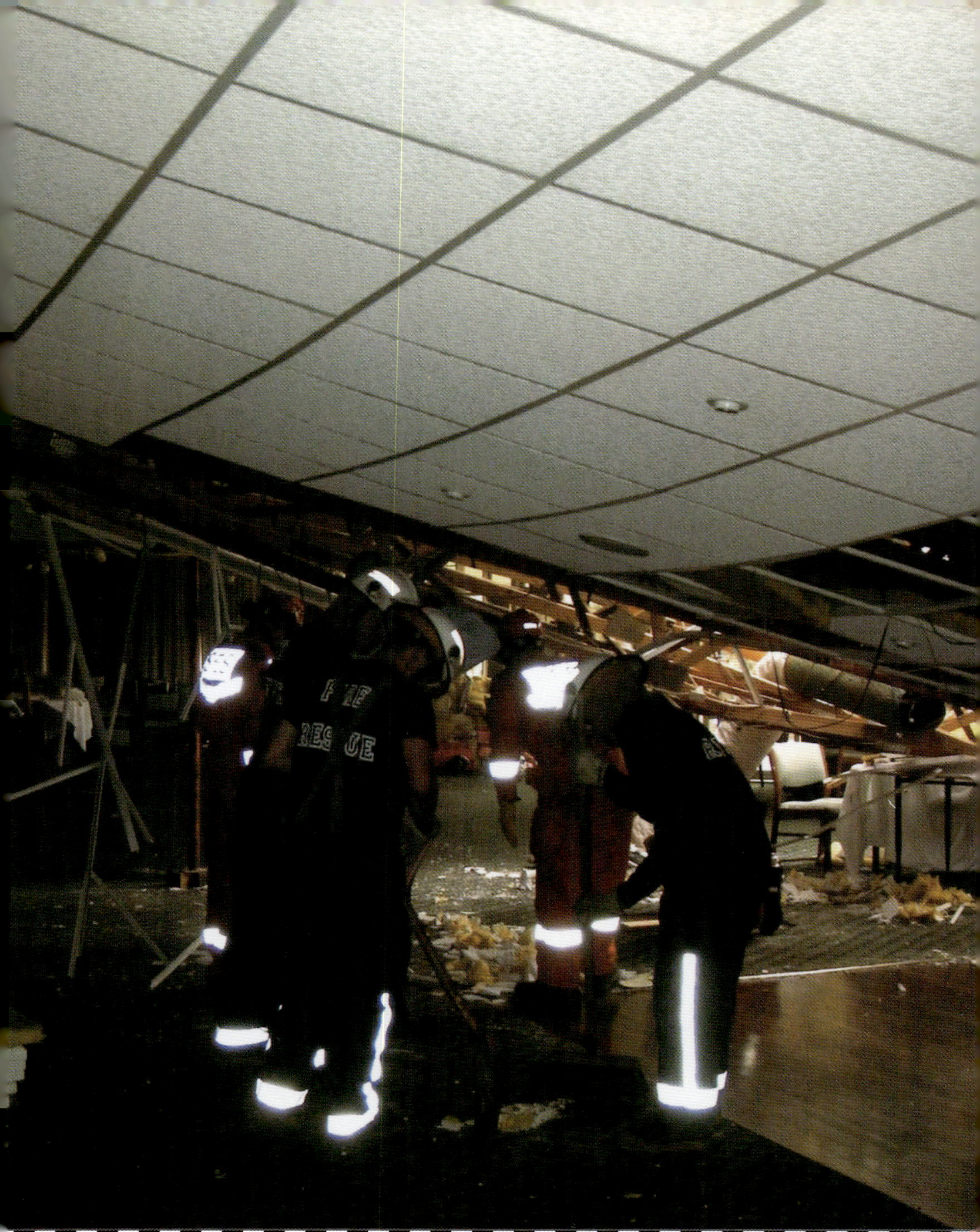

# Other Jobs

Firefighters help at road crashes. A special tool called the "Jaws of Life" is used to free people trapped in cars. It cuts through metal like scissors cut through paper.

Sometimes firefighters are called to help during storms. They also clean up after fires, crashes, and storms.

21

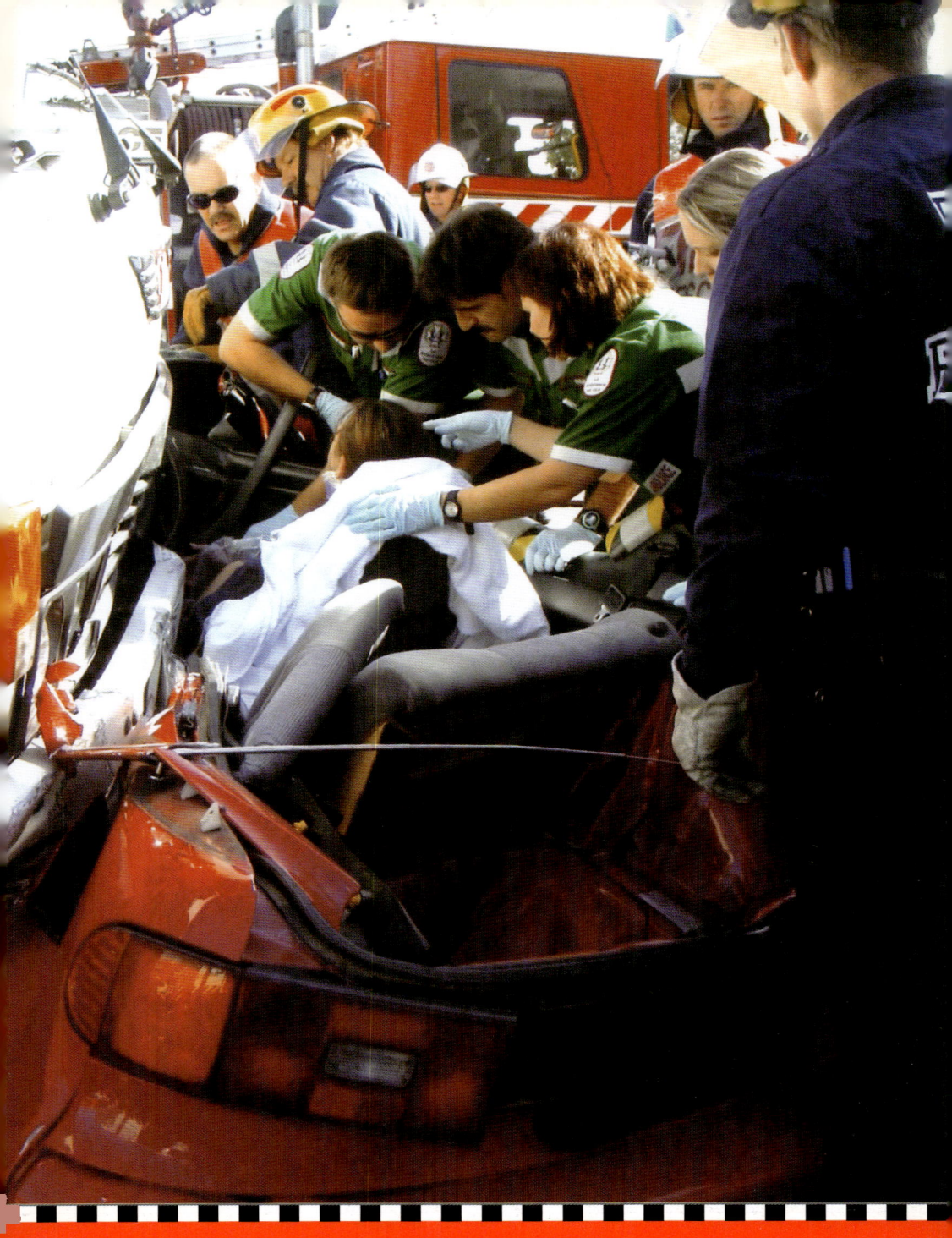

# Education

Firefighters teach people about fire safety. They tell people how to keep their families and homes safe during a fire. They go to schools and talk to children. Some of their messages are:

> Never use fire on your own. Always have an adult handle the fire.
>
> Know two ways out of your house in case of fire. Make an escape plan.
>
> Test your smoke detectors every month and change the batteries twice a year.
>
> Get out of a burning building and stay out. Never go back inside to get anything.
>
> Crawl low under smoke. Smoke rises; the clean air is near the floor.
>
> If your clothes catch on fire, follow these steps: stop, drop, and roll.

23

# Index/Glossary

air tanks 8, 14
ax 10
bandages 12
chemicals 18
community 3
equipment 6, 10, 14
fire extinguishers 14
fire hydrant 10
first aid 6, 12
gas 10
hydrant wrench 10
Jaws of Life 20
oxygen 10
smoke detectors 22
splints 12
wrench 10

**Glossary**
**air tank** a tank filled with air for breathing when needed; it is usually worn on the firefighter's back
**fire extinguisher** a special container of foam, chemicals, or water used for putting out fires
**first-aid kit** a container of commonly used medical supplies
**hydrant** an upright water pipe, usually found along the street
**hydrant wrench** a special tool used to turn on fire hydrants